The Pacific Northwest Poetry Series

Linda Bierds / General Editor

The Pacific Northwest Poetry Series

2001 *John Haines—For the Century's End*

2002 *Suzanne Paola—The Lives of the Saints*

The Lives of the Saints

Suzanne Paola

University of Washington Press

Seattle & London

The Lives of the Saints, the second volume in the PACIFIC NORTHWEST POETRY SERIES, is published with the generous support of CYNTHIA LOVELACE SEARS.

Printed in the United States of America
Designed by Audrey Meyer

06 05 04 03 5 4 3 2 1
First Edition 2002

Library of Congress Cataloging-in-Publication Data
Paola, Suzanne.
The lives of the saints / Suzanne Paola.
p. cm.—(The Pacific Northwest poetry series)
ISBN 0-295-98272-1 (cloth : alk. paper)—ISBN 0-295-98273-X (pbk. : alk. paper)
1. Christian saints—Poetry. 2. Women—Poetry. I. Title. II. Series.
PS3566.A594 L49 2002
811'.54—dc21

2002069579

The paper used in this publication is acid free and recycled from 10 percent post-consumer and at least 50 percent pre-consumer waste. It meets the minimum requirements of American National Standard for Information Sciences—Permanence of Paper for Printed Library Materials, ANSI 239-48-1984.

This book is for St. Christopher

But if I was born in sin and guilt was with me already when my mother conceived me, where, I ask you, Lord, where or when was I, your servant, ever innocent?

—*St. Augustine*

But I want to seek out a means of going to heaven by a little way, a way that is very straight, very short, and totally new.

We are living now in an age of inventions, and we no longer have to take the trouble of climbing stairs, for, in the homes of the rich, an elevator has replaced these very successfully. I wanted to find an elevator which would raise me to Jesus.

—*St. Thérèse of Lisieux*

If they wanted to know about man, why not work on man?

—*Deposition of Dr. Carl Heller*
on the origins of the Human Radiation Experiments

Contents

Prologue

St. Theresa of Avila tells us we must find saints to be our companions, because we need the friendship of those who once had mortal bodies and now do not—*not just the company of those of the angelic orders*, who may not understand.

Saints meaning those-we-know-are-in-heaven. The ones who can plead our case. With the *beati*, their not-quite-sainted kin. Fixed points in our restless stellar cartography.

Like St. Thérèse of Lisieux, the young nun who loved the holy face of Jesus and also chocolate éclairs, who died of tuberculosis at twenty-four. Creator of the spiritual Little Way and unnoticed by her Sisters: poor at sweeping.

St. Catherine, the illiterate medieval self-starver, self-scourger, who learned her letters as a young woman from her bridegroom Christ. And lived to berate popes before dying from anorexia and bulimia.

They were all strength and all nothingness. Invisible: slipping in and out: changing the rules. Like the blank smoke of industrialization. By-product of the machinery of the spirit.

"When reading the lives of the saints," wrote Thérèse, "I was puzzled to see how Our Lord would caress certain ones from the cradle to the grave . . . the ones who had offended him, whom he forced to accept his graces."

The lives of the saints as absurd, evidence of a governing and exuberant caprice. Capable-of-intercession: search engines that stop where we point. The thirty-six righteous ones of the Jews, who keep humankind going: without them the whole armistice that is the world would collapse.

St. Augustine said, "There are three times, a present of past things, a present of present things, and a present of the future." He said, "Otherwise, how do prophets see the future, if there is not yet a future to be seen?"

In the present of past things her spine opens to the bone, white as fossil.

In the present of past things her throat gives a blood-alms to the thin napkin.

Thérèse: *I will return! I will return! My heaven will be spent on earth.*

Their lives a breaking-point, a whirligig of matter.

The lives of the saints take place all around us, under us, so much of the earth they seethe in it like anything else humankind puts there. We find them in our white teeth and as dust mites in the sheets we use, allergen to our dreaming.

In the three times in which we live, in pieces.

This book is written as a polyphony, a chorus spoken about saints and, perhaps occasionally, by them.

to build friendships [perhaps] *with those who have had a mortal body . . .*

The Lives of the Saints

The Lives of the Saints

When I first learned about atoms in high school
nothing seemed more ridiculous than life
if that's all it was: tiny, disintegrating, empty, all-the-same.
Dustdots streaming
toward an even larger collapse.
Everywhere. My mother in her pinkchecked party apron
spun in bits to the dining room, a duck nucleused
by *Joy of Cooking* sauce l'orange in her arms.

& my lubehaired dad crisping the *Tribune* down
to come to her.
He was something else totally,
really just a bundle of nervous hoops.

He knew my mother as small
already, the TV
blaring *I love ya little cutie but the office is my duty*
as legions of husbands left their wives onscreen.

What I saw kept showing me
its rounding Ferris wheels of movement, its poor parts.

At Mary Star of the Sea High School, 5th period science class
it got hard to believe in anything, seeing it all
as the same at the root—
one or two dots' difference, carbon's diamond,
or bound with other, almost identical
atoms, it's me.

Then 7th period Religion we read about
the lives of the saints, so it was like
hearing them try to yank the absurdity to something else.

Or maybe the saints knew it
too, Catherine
with her puslicking, her meals of vomiting & celery.

I loved those people & their comic gestures.
Rose of Lima rubbing pepper on her skin, Jerome
turning restlessly on his nails
showed their indifference to the state of matter.

They were the first atomic scientists.
Francis' parents
cast him off, Rose's too, saints blew up
the world around them.
Like they had to start that way, freed electrons,
so the way in front of them could be clear.

Later I saw them all the time
when my mother grew their look.
I say *grew*. It emerged, a new life, from her face.
The one where you smile & it's real
but the rest of your face does something else completely.

Looks beyond the room, your eyes heavy
with the weight of two existences.

It seemed my mother's cancer hungered for her eyes.
A soft round on the ovary, larger than the organ
it consumed.

They took out everything, the first plushed bed
of my babyhood. "All gone," says my mother
then tells me how she bled, "like
saffron threads" (Indian cooking
with Craig Claiborne, a phase of hers).

She took to eating bacon & eggs & liver.
She's had her thyroid & appendix removed
& tells me she feels like a bladder or balloon, a skin
clung to a wind that's blowing her clean.

After chemo I set her hair the way she likes it, the strands
cytoxin didn't gobble up.
I trapped them in pink rollers the size of fingers—she used them
on me a few times—they had little spikes all around,

& she'd emerge re-done, scrollheaded,
a fountain of those Jewish scripture-curls.

ℨ

For a while I couldn't justify my love of sweets
with all I knew of the world, it stung
or spun, Catherine
lived years on the Host, & I
took a cake-decorating class and squeezed the icing bag
    straight into my mouth.
It saved me: the frosting
mostly powdered sugar, only heaps of sugar
can make a good form & keep it.
Flavors like chocolate just a whisper of elseness

& my secret love became that sugarshock
of icing, that knock to the jaw,
your tongue & teeth can actually vibrate from it.
Your mind screams *pleasure*
your teeth hit with that corruption nervescream *hurt.*

I made cakes & brought them to my mother
first her favorite flowers like roses & bleeding hearts
then drip bags, syringes, & whatever
they took out of her, I made.
I even made a sheetcake using fondant to mold
the smug, sporebearded face of an oncologist she couldn't stand.

She couldn't eat them & I didn't want her to.
It was a way of seeing her life as holdable, slapstick, nothing
but the sweet inside.

The First Letter of St. Paul to the Clones

Fat sheep—
Dolly
grinds above her legs, stalled
Volkswagen of flesh. Frayed cells
eight years older
than her age, straight for senescence at 3.

She-Abraham—
All her little Isaacs die at birth.

Still with that sheep-smirk, that Ark-old
victory look of the born sacrifice.

Watching you follow her: cows, pigs
with hearts rough as catcher's mitts, bones
like jellied soup, the squashed plates
of your faces, black tongue.
Genes testing perfect though you come out wrong,
if you come, miscarrying,
or so large you kill your mothers pushing through.

It's not the genes your makers
botch, but the expression of your genes they can't control—
Joining in new ways, the recessive ones
triumphantly leapt forward—

Heading out now, new land, new covenant.

Blessed Ludovica Albertoni

Ludovica lived from 1473 to 1533 and was sculpted by Bernini in 1671, after the Vatican declared her beata *or blessed.*

I

Dante visited eternity—a rose,
a white rose, at the center a yellow god.
Each of the blessed a petal, open
in the great yawning morningmouth of the whole.

In the year of our lord two-thousand the rose still blooming
in its cobalt garden
in the garden of the sky

I have pastured there, & come back
to where I was & am, turned ornament . . .
Prone, breast held out in offer, on a rock
replica of the pillow I never used.
A girl. Slack-jawed, drooped, mouth open
on the marble sofa of her ecstasy.

Beata, *an end to war, new shoes* Beata—
heal my body, make my daughter eat

They keep on calling me, these women
who live longer & longer, as their bodies shrink.

From the garden that grows around history
I watch a surgeon's bagged garbage: breast breast breast breast—
So many ways to lose ourselves for Him.

II

I took a rose the color of milk,
bound the thorns to my chest. After a while
I couldn't feel it, so I wound it round the nipples,
felt out where it hurt, bound it again.
Purged the boiled hen they forced me to eat.
This was the way to live forever.

On that inch of time where I swayed then
I learned to watch chronology, a card
you could play to win back. Or lose.
Each day a fresh bite from the loaf. I watched
the sour pug-nosed Michelangelo
hammer his Mary & Christ.
                                        Her girlish breasts,
so high & round—*Michael's Melons*, boys laughed,
& the man chiseled his signature between them.
Brunelleschi domed, the Shakespeares
mumbled ghost stories by the Avon River.

My way was a woman's. Dark robe, white veil.
Hunger. Giving away all I had, touching
the reeking purple eggs in the necks of the sick.
All through the years of plague I sopped its yolk.
Surviving, somehow—
Every desire I had I desired off
as evidence of myself. I cleaned my trail
like a murderer.
                            Half-
starved, selfless, penniless, erased.
Chaste, if possible. Silent. Where's Ludovica?
Not here, not here.

III

Eternity, immortality.
To take death apart, heave its stones apart,
pry out & scatter its moss foundation stones
like a flimsy house on valuable fields.
Here's human life in sum. Vague, profane,
but full of longing for more
of whatever it is. What pain it is,
our nerves cry out for it. I whipped myself.

Bernini, admirer of Michelangelo—
Luigi his brother, banished
for *servicing himself of a stableboy*
by the horse of Constantine:
dishonoring the marble of the Vatican.
To buy a pardon Bernini sculpted me.

I came back, in frozen resurrection,
my body, for the first time, sexual.
Hand offering a breast, like Roman Charity,
the girl who nursed her father on her milk.

IV

On my inch of time, on the inch after,
we played the card of art. We altered surface.
Now it's the card of substance. Meddling
at the heart of things. Year two-thousand.
Epoch twenty-one, the end of adolescence,
time to go into the Father's business.
Dolly in her pen, whose wool is wool,
whose spirit's an afterimage, like a blow
to the eyes would leave.

A blur. Though her wool is wool. And men
can weave it. Maybe into a hundred little hats
each with a rosette of wool at the crown
purled to resemble the not-sheep's tail . . .

How atoms once held, like heaven
before Lucifer, the neutron
that was Lucifer, fissioning through the universe.

Enrico Fermi
like me, a Roman, Oppenheimer, *become death,*
climbing from one moment to another
on the ladder of chance, *become death*
(not the fall itself but its inevitable by-product)
the ladder of *once we knew we could do it we had to do it*
become death
the rose blooms over the mushroom, in a ground flattened
    & made rich.

V

Not the fall itself but the matter of the fall . . .
Ores teased to quickness, half-lives.
(Cesium-135, 6 million years
Uranium-238, 10 billion years)
The language of immortality & judgment
& purgatorial fire.

In New Mexico, in '45, the Trinity test.
Sagebrush, cattle, & first atomic bomb.
Oppenheimer borrowed the trinity's name,
a pun, for its trinity of human makers—
at Hanford, Oak Ridge, Alamagordo—
& for its battering will (*three-person'd God*).

After the blast & the ash, creatures,
for miles around, went bald; fur grew back
patched—dogs, cats, cows—spotted
as desert hyenas, till the cancers came.

Doctors had a few civilians fed
pieces of fallout, to see what it would do.
Their stomachs glowed like the burning lips
of desert saints.

VI

I am myself
atomic: mass
turned impulse, a history blown into the sky—
To the wind, in the matter-
mauling twenty-first century, when nuclear dreck
becomes my sister, living,
like me, past
what anything human might endure.

The Waste Isolation Project, Yucca Mountain,
The Waste Isolation Pilot Plant, New Mexico,
All the half-
saints, caged in their desert
watch.
          Signs—

DO NOT COME NEAR UNTIL AD 12,000
by a poster of a bald man vomiting.
A child's cartoon of radiation sickness.
Because who then will read English? Poison
longis, lingua
brief.

VII

Death, on the one hand: what we leave behind
on the other—
this planet like a junkman's attic; we watch
& watch the hoarding, we who are removed.

A Hanford man unspaded twelve tanks
in '98, lightly buried, lightly bleeding plutonium.
Enough to build twelve atomic weapons.
One for each tribe of Israel, one
for each sliver of the sky.

Traces in the salmon, wheat, even the milk there—

I baked my money into brown bread & gave it to the poor.
Some loaves with nothing, some dense with scudi
so God could divide my wealth.

I remember the child, a little girl, she had slept in dung
it was on her face & hands—
who had eyes like a sheep's, full of milky wariness.
She took a soft roll (*grazie Madre*)
                                        & doubled over coughing,
choking, livid then pale, like she would die, finally
someone pounded her back & she coughed up a gold scudo,
looked at me accusingly, flung it into the street.

VIII

Because eternity is a rose
is up, is risen, is present & past
time lends no shadows where we look: I am there
& here, the Light eternal
shines everywhere at once:

Think of a round room frescoed with history,

though it's only history to the flea
stuck onto the paint. From the center out,
from the rose, it runs together—

Uranium is plutonium is itself,
                                                  the breast
bobs on & off the woman's body
so it may be just the boy who plays Juliet
in Shakespeare's theater, who gets up
after stabbing himself, removes his breasts, & eats.

The Second Letter of St. Paul on the Human Genome Project

I sound harder on you than I mean—
You never did anything but what your forty-six chromosomes
cried out for, in their carhorn piston voices.
Up where I am we can hear them, 4 billion of you
& the rauc rising: more & more.
From the first murder, gentle Neanderthal (Abel)
slaughtered by Homo sapiens (Cain). You did
what we asked you to do.
We put mammals in front of your eyes
& you switched from grasses to meat, cheek teeth
sunk like medieval towers crumbled
in the Age of Reason. As soon as you knew
fire you fire-hunted, burning forests to take the few
whatever that might run out to you.
You've never been gentle, is what I mean, & your gentler nature
you forget as quickly as your gods. Whom you make,
slap into the sky & then let fall.
"Prophets have never enjoyed a Darwinian
edge," the biologist said, & those of us here can't pull you out
anymore, of your bodies; you've mapped them well, & you
love those twists & ends.

Patient 6

> *From August 1946 to January 1947, the University of Rochester conducted toxicity studies on uranium, using hospital patients as subjects. Highly enriched uranium (uranium–234 and uranium-235) was administered intravenously.*
>
> —Department of Energy Roadmap
> Human Radiation Experiments

Studies, Investigation, Research

The premise of science: There must be more.
The premise of art: There must be more.
The premise of history: More. More. More.

Deep in this brief & unsupportive body
where dissectors' knives first parsed the slub & ooze,
the sacs where blood's squeezed, the lobes
where fluid taints or air's thinned or.
Or. What goes in
comes out stripped, stinking.

In the Renaissance the body's back
as Idea. It's still soul they seek, that second appendix,
slack bag waiting for the immaculate invisible to come.

What the body consumeth cannot be said
to profit thereby

one dissector writes, sick
with the carnival tangle of intestine & that's
disappointing but not too terribly (there's More)
in the cardiocentric or craniocentric body (nobody's sure
where soul's couched). Leonardo
sketching the optic nerves, almost
as an afterthought.

The search is on. Some cadavers
coming to the dissecting table oddly gouged & warm.

HP6

The purpose of the studies was to determine the dose level at which renal injury is first detectable. . . . Human subjects included four males and two females, all with good kidney function, ranging in age from 24 to 61 years.

All had medical conditions, such as undernutrition, alcoholism, or heart disease.

Flash. Dr. Samuel Bassett's "production
line" (he calls it). He searches
ERs at Christmas to keep the holidays from slowing him.
Looking for the subjects he calls, for the experiment,
Human Products: HP1, HP2, HP3 . . .
The point (More): to see how much radioisotope
the human kidney holds.

("He was not a ghoul," Dr.
Patricia Durbin said. "He was a scientist.")

The HPs hallucinating, malnourished, good enough.
HP (Patient) 6 he-who-gets-most
at 71 micrograms per kilo, up from the 6
where Bassett started

to find that dose of soluble uranium salt which, when introduced
intravenously as a single dose, would produce just detectable

renal injury

Browne, Tyndall, Watters

Sir Thomas Browne, tireless experimenter, torched a flower
heated the char & saw the flower's "very forme and idea"
rise in a bluish smoke above the ash. "Palingenesis," he wrote,
"the reindividuality of an incinerated thing."

Physicist John Tyndall did the same
using acid fumes: he formed apples & tiny fish,
a serpent whose smoke-tongue rolled from the beaker at him.
Wondering at the spirits who live in the bright stung spaces
we can't see. In the '40s Dr. Watters

killed grasshoppers with ether in a cloud chamber,
photographing death's condensation, seeing
the freed, etheric shapes of grasshoppers.
He declared the soul photographable & real, existing
in our intra-atomic spaces, a use
for the voids, a charge.

So Far Away, Patient 6

We rang in 2000 defusing bombs, she says to him (they
have nothing to do with this really, they're just two people).
Everybody wanting
to blow up everything. Oklahoma City, World Trade.
We can't trust fertilizer
or planes. I feel like we climbed the long circular staircase
of the century to get to the top, only
the castle's collapsed. Do we go back down? To where?

Our muse *is* violence (he muses). Just bored, aren't we?
I mean it, she says. Don't you remember? The '63 World's Fair,
  the House
of 2000, robot maids. Aquafarming
that ends hunger, living on the moon. World peace. Endless
cheap clean power from nuclear stations. End of disease. I think
everybody's going crazy seeing the same old shit around.

He shifts his eyes through the Club. This relentless woman
doesn't interest him anymore . . . he sighs & Patient 6
hangs in the room, chimera
of his vapor, his little man.

Or maybe 6 is in the House of 2000, a speck
cycling in and out of the apron-wearing robot vacuum cleaner.

Later

Patient 6, one of the best of the "humble, mild and
conforming" subjects. ("I would avoid the word *experiment*
in this circumstance. Suggest *study, investigation, research . . .*")

Patient 6. After the first bout
of renal failure Bassett tests the theory
that an acid body will love uranium.
Injecting ammonium chloride to induce acidosis,
then another 56
micrograms/kilo of U_6. He's right: *the urinary excretion of
uranium had fallen*

(Doc Durbin: "It's not for the humble to go asking
the established scientist about the motivations for this and that.")

So this then: maybe decalcifying would "liberate some uranium"
from the bone. Calcium's lowered. It
doesn't work. Some U_6, maybe 20%, always lingers in the bone
anyway, bound to the phosphates there, smooching its neutrons
around.

Easter Day in Rochester

HP6 goes into the liquor store, orders Wild Turkey Lucky Strikes &
gum
He shares his grate of course (it's Rochester!) they know him
HP7 HP8 HP9. Can we
have a swig, they ask, HP6 being
a good guy, never a whiner
like some of the other radioactive Human Products the hospital
produced.

His bones crawling with enriched uranium
zinging out the hollows where Watters' soul resides.

Patient 6 as Paul Celan Would Have Uncovered Him

Black milk of pitchblende he drinks it all day
the dripline in the arm the baggie that bloats & falls
A doctor comes in Bic pen crawling on clipboard chart
Your catalase your creatinine your protein-
uria your stung eyes & strawing hair Patient 6.

Dr. Durbin

Dr. Patricia Durbin, the humble
scientist. She once
scrubbed test tubes for Dr. Hamilton, who injected
plutonium into people &, careless with it, died himself.
Durbin who uncovered, later, all the files,
& found what subjects she could
only to test them further, who said
she sometimes wished she hadn't
because of all the fuss—

Almost a sort of memorial rather than something to be ashamed of,
she said, and

They were always on the lookout for somebody who had some kind of terminal disease

seeing them all as glory-givers, angels
bearing a scythe & a crown.

Back at the Club

Did I mention the name? It's *21.*
A funny place, half like something
on a screen (pulsing in tiny parts), half real.
Photos all over in the pixel light: a map,
a boy in a black coat, a sheep.

Dr. Bassett's there, with his high haircut & frowny lips.
Dr. Browne in pleats, lace, trowel of a beard, Leonardo,
Tyndall, Watters. Dr. Durbin
who's drawn to me, woman to woman—

I sit with them at a round table. We all fit in, even
Leonardo in his tights, because it's the end of history,
& what's not Now is Tomorrow or Retro or Goth
or Nostalgia. At the other end of the room a man & a woman
turn from each other without moving, stuck
in the intractable glue of dead conversation.

There's a shape in the room, something we begin to see
not in the glazed mirrors but the air itself. Less real
even than the place, more than thought, not thing.
It's not a shape like a man—that would be too easy.
We all have something in front of us, sketching or measuring wildly
but we can't make it come clear, & we all go home.

Patient 6 as This Author Has Failed to Find Him

I looked for him. I went into each document as if it were a room.
Moved the furniture of all that language
out of the way, to where he crouched (I thought) tense, wary,
panting to be found (I thought)
so much more than this (*White male, aged 61 years. Ht. 163 cm.,*
Wt. 55.2 kg. B.P. 250/84, alcoholism
chronic, chronic pulmonary fibrosis, symptoms suggestive of a gastric
lesion)

I mean physically almost: I poked
what I could find of the body, all the softnesses
where fingers fit, then
combusted the ash, waiting for the form to rise.

My palingenetical man, the one
whose veins bobbed like bluefish to the rod.

Who Senator Markey in '86 labeled "American nuclear guinea pig"
and a reporter searched for, wanting a real name.
Who lives in the pages of the *Journal of Nuclear Medicine,* the
    Boston Herald, the *Albuquerque Tribune.* More than a man
    now, & less.

A *study,* a *research,* an *investigation* a vapor
a message-in-the-sky a proof. Reborn

as the number of incompletion, one less than infinity
waiting for the last addition that makes it all.

The First Letter of St. Paul to the Columbines

Fifteen white crosses on a hill (a field
of strange wheat). & women came
(like to the empty tomb), cut two crosses
up. For Klebold & Harris, the little ones
who said *peekaboo*
& shot,
who no one wished
to blossom from the ground.

Oh mothers of Columbine
in your gray sweatpants, you bear
the dead cross in your arms: weak
corpus of white wood. Stupefied,
as there's another more looped &
virtual world

where all this can go backward—
Where's the simulcast, the screen to shrink it?

How we forget now: the Real World bleeds.
And still glides steady
into that other order. No blood-dipped napkin
held to an ulcered breast, no long vigil for the miracle
in pixel-time. Broadcast
& the roses heaped like a dress slipped off
a transfiguring body,
massed at a schoolyard gate, under the pierced petals of the name.

& here's a Web altar for Cassie,
who might have said *yes I do, I believe*
when Klebold said Is God there
(or maybe another girl said yes, we'll decide
how to play it)
—*Post Your Pledge Yes I Believe for the Unlikely*
Modern-Day Martyr—
in the new two-dimensional time. She's dead
only on one side of the board.
Crime posted same day, a game you can follow
over & over, moving the pieces (scarlet dots marked K & H)
  through the rooms:
library office cafeteria, yellow dots for the injured red dead &
  the green
witnesses only.

Caterinati

All the way to heaven is heaven.
—St. Catherine of Siena (1347-1380)

Her followers were called Caterinati, or else the Beautiful Brigade.

Lily

When I say there was a normal world I stepped back into
I mean I could almost see the door:
a glass door, a doorknob of cold crystal,
a door swung wide by eating yellow cake.
(Not the fishing weights I once sewed in the hem
of my pants. Not the cup after
cup of water.) Once I walked through
I saw how absurd I'd been on the other side of it,
a loose wire in sweatpants, wingbones
jutting from my cheeks, my face wanting to fly off.

It astonishes me: there are so many normal people.
Without thinking much they put on their normal clothes
that serve as a warm introduction to one another.
And their fat furniture & humped
cars. They don't
have to think about it they just
like the same things. The kind of TV
where people are moving bones with a light jelly on them
& they meet in restaurants & quip & eat. Or rather
they order steaks & half chickens, chew
one well-amplified bite, & laughingly go home.

That's not real, my doctor says, but I watch
the real, offscreen tables of untouched meat.

About Catherine

"Always mostly immersed in the supernatural"
living survivor of a dead twin, her long hair
the blond of milkfat,
at twelve she takes her father the dyer's scissors & flut flut flut
the fall scirocco's a sneeze of hair—
Her mother takes her to a hot spring: she finds one
that's 200° & bubbles holes in her skin.
Now that she's mineral she'll no longer eat.

Only God can marry me after this, she says, thinking God
takes what he gets, not choosy.

Then comes the three years in her little cell
at home, the mechanical
raising & lowering of her arm, its brief
whip-tentacle. Like she was
a gizmo, a 19th-century
itinerant's contraption,
                                        the brass monkey's arm
shoveling its throat with coin.

Madame M.

The hair shirt. The spiked girdle & the iron chain.
Herself dom
& sub, fantasy & fulfillment.

We call ourselves *players* & in the animal world
play is always a predatory act. Who leads, who
feeds? The one who gives pain
knows precisely what to give, the one who takes
plays the minor chords of his body as he wants to.
He will call me *Mistress* a word that is power & powerlessness
like *saint.*

I have a den with an oak Magnavox I lock away
& then I throw open a cupboard & call it
dungeon. It's always
the powerful men who want this, & they're exact.
Losing control the way an architect dynamites
a building, so it falls
this way. In dog collar, nipple clamp, cuffs & rope
like each piece of what you are must be separately stopped.

Lily

She chewed & chewed lettuce & celery then spat them out.
Tickled her throat
with a feather, saying
Let's bring the miserable sinners up for judgment. (I
had no arguments, or nothing could have made me eat.)

Wore the Dominican habit & stayed at home
in a nine-foot cell, with her prayers & her beatings, a willed
& shuddering singularity. She sculpted her body down
to the real woman: I always felt
five pounds away from myself.

I remember the deaths of the Kennedys & a woman
named Jeane: she predicted them, & then
blithered on through the next thirty years—
World War III, Russia beating us to the moon.
Cosmic peace & harmony, all
before 2000. Everything & everyone in history
will be right once or twice, like a
stopped clock. & then go lunatic.

Madame M.

I love to garden. No one
believes this. I joke: my plants are black & blue,
& bloodred of course . . .
Not true. I like columbines & cosmos, all the pastelly shades
of innards if you washed them in a sink of milk.
Not roses, with their thorns & rust.
I joke: they're the dominants
of the garden, I won't have competition.
Wrong, they're subs, in control
through their incessant weakness.

Catherine said to the clergy, *you are flowers*
that shed no perfume but stench
I repeated that
to my submissives, they loved it.

Let me read you something—

This the glorious Paul taught you when he said
that you should mortify the body
macerating
the flesh
          whenever it should wish
to combat the spirit, but the will should be
               dead and annihilated in everything, and subject to My will.

In this submission, Catherine writes, is freedom,
& my players call & ask for my nun routine.

Lily

Once when Christ drew her to him
she put her mouth to the wound (real mouth & soul's
mouth) & drank, like a lover or an infant.
A rapture she felt physically, she wrote.
She imagined God marrying us with the divine wedding ring the
Holy Foreskin.
On a peace mission to Florence she prayed for someone to kill her.

Madame M.

This is how it goes: first negotiations, set limits, get
a safeword to stop it all, then
the scene begins. I lurch into my boots
barking, *Face in the dust Worm,*
trying not to remember that's Jeremiah.
Yes: it arouses me: my black boa & needleheeled
boots, their bent glosslipped
obedience: hurting, when I want, the meaty
tender parts. I might pinch them
for biting a pear or put grape juice, chirring
"menstrual blood," to their mouths. They like that.
And always in a room in my mind is their liking it.

I have a fantasy of the time before birth
as negotiation. What can I do to you, he/she says
& we say This, this, not that. In my
tender soul there are these places you may not touch.
So we can rest in a small pool
of our own dissent—
                                        Here's what
you can say to stop me, the Word says, offering a word.

Then we can begin & pretend it's all happening
for the first time.

Catherine Redux: The Mystical Marriage (A Dumbshow)

First we see the pallet on the rush floor with a few straws
stuck out like needles.
David comes, adjusting his harp strings. What he plays
is indescribable so we can't hear it.
Lit up from within, still with that earthly musician's frown
of pain/pleasure. The bride
wears a loose white smock almost carried by her rib bones.

The Virgin Mother gives her boy away. He's tall
& pierced, not the puff-faced baby who married
Catherine of Alexandria. Supported
by his best men, Sts. Paul and Dominic.
She in her black & white habit faints.

The Relationship

After the marriage Jesus would come to her pallet sometimes.
He drew her head lovingly to his bleeding.

She in time like a woman sewn into a bone girdle.
When she cut off her dusty hair she looked feral almost.
Like someone who *could* stick her hand in a fresh wound.

Her confessor Raymond reported her childhood habit
of pausing at each stair to say a *Hail Mary*.
Raymond wrote that angels might pick up her feet
& carry her. At the age of seven she saw Jesus
dressed up as the pope in a backstreet of Siena
over the guttering pigsnouts & urine.

Lily

Before the mystical marriage she lived a year
on the Host only, with a teaspoon of herbs & water—
her body as pure Idea. There was
so little separating her from air—
nothing fell through her mouth to scrape
the borders, make her body real.

One time in the bathroom my mother walked in on me
where I turned around & around on the toilet
to look at myself in the medicine chest mirror—*Christ*
you look like something from Biafra, she said, *two gnawed chicken*
    wings
for legs, who do you think's
going to want you like that? & I thought
so much about her question, how I knew
it had an answer, but didn't know what it was.

There are people whose job it is to mimic the saints
like the mimes who sneak up on pedestrians, stiffly
& excessively mimicking—where an arm swings
with a briefcase the shadow arm
circles emptyhanded in a comic loop.
Seen one way the second man lessens the other.
Seen another way he puts in italics
all that makes the original himself.

So you look again thinking yes that's him—
the cartooning of him making him less a cartoon
of a man with a briefcase than a real man
with stiff elbows, no sense of humor, a vague limp.

Madame M.

I had a client, called himself Jerry,
an older man, scrawny.
When I left the room he'd be whaling away on himself.
Solitary pleasure. Used a piece
called a *Rachel* we bought at the Fetish
Palace. She used a rusted chain. Went
from the hair shirt to an iron girdle. Which of course
thanks to her celerysucking & green water
must have been talking to itself after a while.

Catherine, Finally

Once she sat in a garden with her neck free
from the wimple, & saw martyrdom coming
in the bright blurred garden the knives reflected.
But the men shouldered their blades & left
her with no current to float away on—

She prayed for martyrdom & holes,
a hundred cuts like a hundred rivers
feeding into the estuary of the church on earth.

Madame M.

I know that time—
her drive to be prey,
be color & food at the end.
Not the still dry death she had, heart stopped
simply in a starved body.

She wanted someone else to give her
her body's capacity for pain, beautifully meted out.
I might have loved her then but not enough.

Lily

That spilling, that gagging abundance!
like Jesus, whose wounds, she said
we could dip our bread in—
enough
of herself for everyone to eat.

The Third Letter of St. Paul at the Playground

The deckle edge of sunset folds: a letter
sinks. You see that. Though nobody
writes to you & earth's just a hard ball
revolving. Everything
that is
is matter, even light:
or all matter's light (the wind
knocked out of it).

I look around.
I see packets of atomic
parts, each one
can go *boom boom* or assemble
into these sweet legs shimmying like geese gullets
over Barney sandals. Voices
from the swing caw *Nah Nah Nah*
Poopoo Head, or
peekaboo. A mother says *Destiny*
keep your socks on, so bored & chronic
her voice is like a vacuum sucking in.

She makes a tired wind with one hand.
& I can remember how hard it is
to wait like this, our microscopic parts
doing what they do, & we just umpires
in the game, not players really.
Do they put hard clots in the lung, does a burst
of atomic light knock us off the horse?
Stephen Hawking says space-time's curved
like the North Pole, a place where the child Destiny,
spinning to her bored mother, keeps lisping God lives.

The Lives of the Saints II: Rosette

(Thérèse =St. Thérèse of Lisieux)

The Zepherine Drouhin's impossible to grow—
a martyr to rust, my mother said, when she weighed
eighty-five pounds & her cough rasped,
grinding her bones together. I imagined her
inside, full of a fine white meal. The fierce
chlorophyll of morphine. She had had her hair done
before going in the last time, a head of fat pubic
curls. *Make it last this time,* she said.

When the Zeph. bloomed three weeks in that wet winter
I knew Thérèse held us in her hands.
I began piping perfect shells. The saint
worked with me. The shells
hard white, spined, perfectly articulate.
Impossible for me before.

It's something I can only tell
to her, how much I think about cakes, about frosting,
the white solemn surface—
not wet, not dry, this blank
moisture my hand feeds.
My bud roses, drop flowers, floodwork,
weave, & figure piping, & stars.

A martyr to rust, my mother said of the Zeph., like she
was not the concern.

Sometimes I mix my colors, do flowers
in black gray olive, inner-ear, inner-flower dark.

For my mother's wake: a garden of mudbrown grass,
black satin apple blossoms on black stems, slate roses.
I held a wedding woman to a gas flame, bent her double
& robed her in black buttercream (my sister
took her off), still the cake sat there, a sheet cake,
& a mourning-garden, like what
the vague blue hand of death would plant.

Why shouldn't we take what we can & leave our mark?
God did that, I'm sure, in Genesis
found out what he was
& what he didn't want to be any longer.

I border with rosettes, there, where one universe ends
& another less
personal one begins.

❧

Saint Thérèse
on her own photograph: *yes that's the envelope. When*
will anyone see the letter?

Though it's the envelope we love: a salt-cellar
reliquary of femur, pinch of hair on a cross. At Carmel
the other nuns
crowded her cooling body. A dead virgin, a bellpull
to the Lord! Whether they liked her or not they cupped her feet.
Sister St. Vincent found herself cured of a sucking anemia,
her blood plush as ocean.

If I'da been a saint, my mother said, coughing
(pointing to the tucked skin where her breasts had hung)
you could make a fortune off these . . .

~

I put a cake in the car when I went to see her.
White, with pink roses, a true pink you get
with just a toothpick-tip of Christmas Red.
Fingertip scatter of apple blossom. White rosettes
marking the border. Her relics delivered
from place to place, I expected
a brilliant white limo with rearview rosary dangling
instead she came in a blue stationwagon, New Jersey plates,
bare.
The church calls it the *Thérèsemobile.*

Her riding in the gilt & jacaranda bonebox (Rome won't say
how many bones we got)
plexiglass & under it, rosettes
on the gothic spires. At Our Lady's
they had six little girls with America roses
throw petals in her path.

The long wait in line
& the woman I stood behind tubed
in Ralph Lauren jeans, with gray-blond
cocker spaniel–hair. She held two fists full of rosaries,
touching them to the box in practiced turns—
each side of the crucifix had to touch—
& when she caught my eye she squinted
in a shrugging, humorous but not sorry way . . .

Doing it to sell, I thought, *she must be*, the way
she glanced at the box, the saint's photo
suspended there, without interest.
Rosaries dripping kelplike from her hand.

Won't do anybody any good, my mother said, *not blessed*
that way.

Thérèse's mother like my mother followed her breasts to heaven
but when Thérèse was four not forty, too young
for sponging off bedsores, turning
& turning a body, the letter
slipped halfway out.

I don't use butter in my frosting. Only Crisco. Powdered
sugar, for the whitest
white, of mountaintops & ravished souls. Too sweet

Peter says. Said. I have a theory that if humankind hadn't fallen
we could love that sweetness. How could any joy
be too much?

I used to think I made my cakes
so the eater could know God's glory here on earth,
the beauties earthly things can reach for.

Then my mother felt out her last
metastases, I couldn't conceive, Peter left
by printing out an e-mail he wrote a friend
where he said I had no heart, & bad thighs. He knew,
he wrote, his past had been one gross error. . . then I believed
I could only give a moment's sugary numbness
to a life pointless & without pleasure.

Finally I believed, all at once,
both reasons.

Thérèse in my cottage garden, Thérèse on the freeway
in a box on the backseat, like a cake.

I wanted to find an elevator
which would raise me to Jesus.

What I keep regretting isn't Peter
or the death of my mother
but being a woman who can't keep roses alive—
who prunes in spring, won't deadhead, won't feed
or give weekly water, who might plant thyme
& mow it down with the lawnmower, half careless,
half cruel.
Getting disgusted finally in August & putting down
diazinon & Miracle-Gro.
The deaths of small things
barely worthy of anyone's forgiveness.

Jesus isn't doing much to keep the conversation going
Thérèse said once, a woman who spoke in rose petals.

If she comes to you, you get roses somehow
like my friend Ruth whose tubes ruptured.
Out the ambulance window she saw Thérèse, smiling,
& when she came to
a silk shock of petals in her palm.
Fell off something, the nurse said, *here have it*
—a white rose—
& now Ruth calls the saint *Terry*, like they've been to lunch.

My father said, *She makes sainthood real*
to people like us . . . the mundane, almost
profane martyrdoms & ecstasies

Giving herself, at Carmel, the rustiest spoon
the coldest piece of omelette, offering herself
as a *victim to Merciful Love*, detailing
The Anguish of the Parlor Visits.
Before that at age 14 her Christmas conversion, Jesus
filling her soul as she started to scream
about wanting Christmas presents in her shoes.

The sweet flower of passion she squeezed
from the bag of ordinary life.

ൟ

Peter wanted me to *want*
more for myself, my own shop, a life
with something in it that could pass for glory.

Always beside me at my dinged spot in the kitchen butcher
    block
hovering above my pleasure.
Always taking my tips & spinning them on his thumb.

If I got sick enough of him I snapped the TV on.
Once after my mother's
cytoxin drip (enough to kill
a swarm of locusts, the doctor said,
beyond tact) & my mother probably still vomiting
back there at the hospital, thumbing her
Combatting Cancer with Potent Potions handbook—

Peter & I stood & watched a show on marsupials
me squeezing out budroses & Gerber daisies
Pete spinning, me piping, & between us
the invisible ink of thought . . .

Once in evolutionary time
everything was marsupials, but the earth broke up,
so they survived in Australia—kangaroos, wombats,
koalas—but died out all over the rest.
Still giving birth to embryos they carry in pouches like letters,
too weak, wiped out
on other continents by newer stronger species, & a mother
kangaroo will throw her babe
to the reformed, mammal
body of a dingo, rather than die herself.

(So this is the world You made the first time, You
who feel so unsurprised by it all!)

And I stopped to watch while my #77
star tip went clattering across the floor.

How could this be enough?
That's what he said to me.

The First Letter of St. Paul in the Homogocene

The Holocene ended
in the year 2000, roughly.
Did you feel your feet when you stepped out of it?
Free to touch Kentucky bluegrass in any climate
on the globe. My Master
can menace fig trees on a penthouse terrace in the north.
Wheat in the rainforest, wheat on the steppes.
30,000 species a year blown out.

Birth of the unispecies singular world.
They're calling it homogocene, *sameness-time*, I call it
you (human) & the things you drag
stuck to your leg, that thrive on your relentless
survival: the crabgrass & stripmalls,
rats roaches & crows.

(What grows in the desert this year?)

Carnivorous primate, frail body
in need of much shelter to survive.
Visual linguistic species, shut out
of the smell-sound earth, the sweet dank planet
moles inhabit, the whales'
clickclick cosmos of echoes—
a whole geography invisible to you, falling.

Your prophets cry out to you

As for my people, children will be their oppressors

the human condition baffles all the more because it is both unprecedented and bizarre, almost beyond understanding/an evolutionary abnormality

And it shall come to pass, that instead of sweet smell there shall be stink; and instead of wellset hair baldness; and burning instead of beauty.

& you're deaf to them though they can't stop speaking—
fossil fuel burning at their lips.

Notes

(Page 10) "*servicing himself* . . ." The quote is from the Renaissance *avvisi* in the Vatican archives.

(Page 11) J. Robert Oppenheimer, remembering the first nuclear bomb test, recalled himself thinking this line from the Bhagavad Gita: "I am become death, the destroyer of worlds."

(Page 12) Oppenheimer, when he named the Trinity test, had been reading John Donne's *Holy Sonnet XIV,* which begins, "Batter my heart, three-person'd God."

(Page 14) *scudo:* a coin of Renaissance Italy.

(Page 16) "Prophets have never enjoyed . . ." This quote is from biologist Edward Wilson's essay, "Is Humanity Suicidal?"

(Pages 17, 19) The epigraphs, as well as the internal quotes describing the experiment (*to find that dose,* etc.) come from Dr. Samuel Bassett's original abstract on the experiment, known in the Department of Energy's Human Radiation Experiment (HREX) files as U2.

(Page 19) "He was not a ghoul . . ." quoted in "The Plutonium Experiment," a series of articles by Eileen Welsome in the *Albuquerque Tribune* in November of 1993.

(Page 22) "I would avoid the word *experiment* . . ." memo from Eugene Saenger in regard to preparing a draft document explaining the total body irradiation HREX. Cf. memo from R. S. Paul on another HREX: "in the second sentence of the second paragraph the word 'victims' is unnecessarily troublesome."

(Page 25) *"Almost a sort of memorial. . . . They were always on the lookout . . ."* quoted in "The Plutonium Experiment."

(Pages 30, 31) The quotations describing Catherine's life come from her confessor and biographer, Raymond of Capua.

(Page 34) "You are flowers . . ." Catherine of Siena, *Letters;* "This the glorious Paul . . ." Catherine of Siena, *The Dialogue.*

(Pages 3–6, 44–53) The two "Lives of the Saints" poems share the same fictional speaker.

(Page 50) *"I wanted to find an elevator . . ."* from *Story of A Soul: The Autobiography of St. Thérèse of Lisieux.*

(Page 55) The first and third italic quotations are from Isaiah. The second is from Edward Wilson, "Is Humanity Suicidal?"

This poem owes a conceptual debt to Edward Wilson's book, *The Diversity of Life.*

Acknowledgments

Two of these poems found other homes originally and have had a slight change of clothing or a little haircut between then and now: “The Lives of the Saints II: Rosette” in the *Iron Horse Literary Review;* both “Lives of the Saints” poems in *The Milk of Almonds* (Feminist Press). My thanks to both publishers.

Linda Bierds has been a combination of coach, midwife, and guru, seeing this book through from an early and incomplete assortment of poetry to a finished work, which, with all its faults, will always be far better than it could have been without her. Such editorial care has become rare and precious. Linda, my deepest thanks.

The staff at the University of Washington Press has been a joy to work with: Audrey Meyer, Pat Soden, and Gretchen Van Meter, whom I commend for her careful and true editorial work on this manuscript. Perhaps it takes a bit of a saint to care so for poetry in our age.

To Bruce Beasley: your insight on poetry is almost as vital to me as you are. To Bruce and Jin (the TGG): because without the astonishment of your light it would all be too hard to think about.

Thank you to Brenda Miller and Mary Janell Metzger for keen last-minute readings: always good women to have close by in a pinch.

I owe a huge thanks to someone I do not know: reporter Eileen Welsome, for her series in the *Albuquerque Tribune* exposing the Human Radiation Experiments, and for her wonderful book on the subject, *The Plutonium Files*. She reminds us that in fighting unknown enemies we often wage war on ourselves.

Finally, this book is lovingly dedicated to my brother Chris.

Suzanne Paola is a recipient of the National Endowment for the Arts Literature Fellowship for 2002–2003. She is the author of three award-winning books of poetry, including, most recently, *Bardo.* Her prose memoir, *Body Toxic,* is a *New York Times* Notable Book of the Year for 2001. She lives with her husband and their young son in Bellingham, Washington.

A NOTE ON THE TYPE

The book was set in Minion and Poetica Chancery II. The Minion and Poetica typefaces were designed by Robert Slimbach (b. 1956–), San Francisco, and issued by Adobe in 1989 and 1992. Poetica Chancery, a calligraphic font, is used for display. These fonts are masterful examples of digital design. The typesetting was done by Suzanne Harris at Integrated Composition Systems in Spokane.